JAMES

FAITH IN ACTION

10 Studies for Individuals or Groups

CHUCK & WINNIE CHRISTENSEN

Harold Shaw Publishers • Wheaton, Illinois

CONTENTS

INTRODUCTION

Reading the book of James is like taking a cold shower: uncomfortable but invigorating. Early on James makes it clear that Christians don't have the luxury of believing one way and living another. We must put feet on our faith and love God with our lives. James spurs us on to maturity with practical insights and timely reminders.

This letter was one of the very early epistles circulated among the first-century Christians. This assures us of its importance and practical worth, for James wrote from a unique vantage point. Steeped in knowledge of the Old Testament law and the prophetic writings, he was an important leader in the church at Jerusalem. He watched it develop from one hundred and twenty faithful believers to a congregation numbering thousands. Impressive growth! But just as impressive was the spread of the message to the outskirts of the Roman Empire. Believers scattered by persecution travelled far, witnessing as they went. From the center of the action, James saw the progress.

James wrote out of unusual experiences. He was the brother of Jesus, and recollections of living in the same home with the God-man must have remained strong in his memory. In addition, the expansion of the new church brought the pressing question, "How is this Christianity to be worked out in everyday life?" Much of his ministry must have involved finding answers to that question, prayerfully seeking the wisdom he discusses in his letter.

James wrote with a distinctive style. He was direct. He spoke out sternly about displeasing God. He probed inner attitudes and outward actions. He punctuated his concern with a repetition of important ideas.

James wrote to people like us—with similar fears, doubts, and hardships—and this letter is a bridge from the first-century believers to today's Christians. He affirms that Christianity can work in a world that includes both rich and poor; where instability is the rule of the day; where the cutting power of speech is felt in the mass media and over the backyard fence; where the excitement of the competitive, commercial world beckons for attention; where the inner staleness of Christians allows them to drift from the Lord. He has something important to say to all of us.

But after James has had his say, we know he still loves us, and that he longs for us to live up to the truth we find in the perfect "law that gives freedom." He urges us to be impartial, to pray, visit, love, and sing. James wants to lead us in active allegiance to the Lord Jesus Christ in both thought and deed until we see our faith expressed in action.

HOW TO USE THIS STUDYGUIDE

Fisherman studyguides are based on the inductive approach to Bible study. Inductive study is discovery study; we discover what the Bible says as we ask questions about its content and search for answers. This is quite different from the process in which a teacher *tells* a group *about* the Bible and what it means and what to do about it. In inductive study God speaks directly to each of us through his Word.

A group functions best when a leader keeps the discussion on target, but this leader is neither the teacher nor the "answer person." A leader's responsibility is to *ask*—not *tell*. The answers come from the text itself as group members examine, discuss, and think together about the passage.

There are four kinds of questions in each study. The first is an *approach question.* Used before the Bible passage is read, this question breaks the ice and helps you focus on the topic of the Bible study. It begins to reveal where thoughts and feelings need to be transformed by Scripture.

Some of the earlier questions in each study are *observation questions* designed to help you find out basic facts—who, what, where, when, and how.

When you know what the Bible says you need to ask, *What does it mean?* These *interpretation questions* help you to discover the writer's basic message.

Application questions ask, *What does it mean to me?* They challenge you to live out the Scripture's life-transforming message.

Fisherman studyguides provide spaces between questions for jotting down responses and related questions you would like to raise in the group. Each group member should have a copy of the studyguide and may take a turn in leading the group.

A group should use any accurate, modern translation of the Bible such as the *New International Version,* the *New American Standard Bible,* the *Revised Standard Version,* the *New Jerusalem Bible,* or the *Good News Bible.* (Other translations or paraphrases of the Bible may be referred to when additional help is needed.) Bible commentaries should not be brought to a Bible study because they tend to dampen discussion and keep people from thinking for themselves.

SUGGESTIONS FOR GROUP LEADERS

1. Read and study the Bible passage thoroughly beforehand, grasping its themes and applying its teachings for yourself. Pray that the Holy Spirit will "guide you into truth" so that your leadership will guide others.

2. If the studyguide's questions ever seem ambiguous or unnatural to you, rephrase them, feeling free to add others that seem necessary to bring out the meaning of a verse.

3. Begin (and end) the study promptly. Start by asking someone to pray for God's help. Remember, the Holy Spirit is the teacher, not you!

4. Ask for volunteers to read the passages out loud.

5. As you ask the studyguide's questions in sequence, encourage everyone to participate in the discussion. If some are silent, ask, "What do you think, Heather?" or, "Dan, what can you add to that answer?" or suggest, "Let's have an answer from someone who hasn't spoken up yet."

6. If a question comes up that you can't answer, don't be afraid to admit that you're baffled! Assign the topic as a research project for someone to report on next week.

7. Keep the discussion moving and focused. Though tangents will inevitably be introduced, you can bring the discussion back to the topic at hand. Learn to pace the discussion so that you finish a study each session you meet.

8. Don't be afraid of silences: some questions take time to answer and some people need time to gather courage to speak. If silence persists, rephrase your question, but resist the temptation to answer it yourself.

9. If someone comes up with an answer that is clearly illogical or unbiblical, ask him or her for further clarification: "What verse suggests that to you?"

10. Discourage Bible-hopping and overuse of cross-references. Learn all you can from *this* passage, along with a few important references suggested in the studyguide.

11. Some questions are marked with a ♦. This indicates that further information is available in the Leader's Notes at the back of the guide.

12. For further information on getting a new Bible study group started and keeping it functioning effectively, read Gladys Hunt's *You Can Start a Bible Study Group* and *Pilgrims in Progress: Growing through Groups* by Jim and Carol Plueddemann.

SUGGESTIONS FOR GROUP MEMBERS

1. Learn and apply the following ground rules for effective Bible study. (If new members join the group later, review these guidelines with the whole group.)

2. Remember that your goal is to learn all that you can *from the Bible passage being studied.* Let it speak for itself without using Bible commentaries or other Bible passages. There is more than enough in each assigned passage to keep your group productively occupied for one session. Sticking to the passage saves the group from insecurity and confusion.

3. Avoid the temptation to bring up those fascinating tangents that don't really grow out of the passage you are discussing. If the topic is of common interest, you can bring it up later in informal conversation following the study. Meanwhile, help each other stick to the subject!

4. Encourage each other to participate. People remember best what they discover and verbalize for themselves. Some people are naturally shyer than others, or they may be afraid of making a mistake. If your discussion is free and friendly and you show real interest in what other group members think and feel, they will be more likely to speak up. Remember, the more people involved in a discussion, the richer it will be.

5. Guard yourself from answering too many questions or talking too much. Give others a chance to express themselves. If you are one who participates easily, discipline yourself by counting to ten before you open your mouth!

6. Make personal, honest applications and commit yourself to letting God's Word change you.

JOYFUL PERSEVERANCE

James 1:1-4

"Life is difficult," observes Dr. Scott Peck in his book *The Road Less Traveled*. It's an obvious fact, right? Yet unannounced, painful problems often whirl us into a dazed panic or angry resentment. In the opening of his letter, James acknowledges that life is indeed difficult. But he challenges his readers to look deeper, assuring them that God is involved in the whole of life, working for our growth and our good.

1. How do you usually respond to unexpected changes in your life?

Read James 1:1-4.

2. How does the author identify himself in verse 1? Keeping in mind his background, what does this say about James?

◆ 3. James mentions Jesus by name only twice in his letter (1:1 and 2:1). What is the significance of each aspect of the title James gives to Jesus?

◆ 4. To whom is this letter addressed (verse 1)? Who would be included in this audience (see Acts 8:1, 4; 11:19-21)?

5. What kinds of trials and difficulties would these people be facing as they settled into new communities?

6. What is James's radical suggestion for facing trials and handling stress (verse 2)? On what basis can we accept trials in this way?

7. What does a tested faith produce (verse 3)? What does this mean?

8. What would happen to our faith if it were never tested?

9. What is God's goal in the life of every believer (verse 4)?

What does it mean to you to be "complete, not lacking anything"?

10. Define *perseverance*. What keeps you from persevering in your walk of faith?

11. Take time to pray for renewed trust and joy in the midst of difficulties.

STEADY UNDER STRESS

James 1:5-18

It's the end of the month, and you don't have enough money to cover the bills. A tragedy has hit your life, and you're not sure what you believe about God anymore. Your daughter is angry and rebellious. Your boss harasses you at work. You lose your struggle against temptation and rationalize your choices. The car breaks down and has to be in the shop for a week. Stresses of daily life go on and on, some large and painful, others just needling inconveniences. How can we walk in faith through hard times? James tells us a way to regain our spiritual perspective by keeping a steady eye on our loving Father, who promises us rich wisdom and blessings as we trust him in stressful situations.

1. What motivates you the most to complete a long-term project or difficult goal?

Read James 1:5-18.

    2. What is the first thing we should do when we are perplexed (verse 5)? What is *wisdom*?

    3. What does verse 5 tell us about God?

◆ **4.** What warning does James give in verses 6-8? When we doubt, what are we saying to God?

    5. What is the "high position" a poor person enjoys (verse 9)?

    6. What does James say a wealthy person should rejoice in (verse 10)? Why?

7. In what ways can the pressures of *poverty* or of *wealth* affect a Christian's attitude toward God?

8. What are we supposed to do when difficulties don't let up (verse 12)?

What would be some advantages of quitting? Some disadvantages?

◆ **9.** What is promised to the one who perseveres? What else motivates the Christian to endure (verse 12)?

10. What excuse do people sometimes make for giving in to temptation (verse 13)? Why is it unthinkable to blame God?

11. According to verse 14, where does temptation begin?

What is the end result of uncontrolled sinful desire (verse 15)?

12. Rather than enticing us to evil, what does God do for the believer (verse 17)? What phrases in this verse describe the kind of God we have?

♦ **13.** What are some of God's perfect gifts to you? What is the ultimate aim of his goodness?

LISTENING AND DOING

James 1:19-27

Obedience is often viewed as something nice and necessary for children or dogs, but stifling for individuality and highly valued independence. James takes issue with this line of thinking. As Christians we are called to humbly accept what we hear in God's Word and put our faith into action. Rather than restricting us, this obedience results in our living with freedom and blessing.

1. What do you think characterizes a "good listener"?

Read James 1:19-27.

2. How will the commands given in verse 19 help us to develop spiritual maturity?

3. What can anger never accomplish? Why not?

4. How is *accepting* the word different from merely *listening* to it (verse 21)? What habits hinder our accepting it?

5. Listening to the word is only the first step. Applying the illustration in verses 23-24, what happens if we don't act on what we hear?

♦ **6.** What is identified as the "mirror" in verse 23? In what way is the Word of God liberating?

7. What does perseverance mean in this context?

Contrast the results in the lives of the mere listener and the one who puts into practice what he or she has heard (verses 22, 25).

8. What do you think of when you describe a person as "religious"?

9. How does James describe a truly devout person (verses 26-27)?

♦ **10.** What does it mean to keep from being "polluted by the world"?

11. Why do you think these three areas of life (verses 26-27) are important to God the Father?

12. Think of instances when you have paid only momentary attention to God's message (e.g., the last sermon you heard; the last time you read the Bible for yourself). Why did you fail to put it into practice? Ask God for help in taking steps to obey what you hear.

LOVING WITHOUT JUDGING

James 2:1-13

If we are honest, we must admit that we want to see ourselves as "better" than the next person. As this portion of James's letter indicates, judging and discriminatory attitudes have always been a problem—inside and outside God's family. The young and growing Christian church, made up of believers "scattered among the nations," was comprised of various ethnic groups, nationalities, religious backgrounds, and social classes. Favoritism toward the rich, the prestigious, and the powerful had to be dealt with lest the body of Christ became like just another social club or political organization. As we read the exhortations to these early Christians, we would be wise to take a look at our own attitudes—and our own, present-day churches. As our faith operates in response to the needs and pressures of society, God will be achieving his goals within us.

1. Have you ever experienced discrimination? How did it affect you?

Read James 2:1-13.

2. What standard is set in verse 1? Why is showing favoritism incompatible with faith in Jesus Christ?

3. Paraphrase verses 2-3 in a contemporary setting. How do you respond to people who do not fit into patterns that you think are appropriate?

4. According to verse 4, what are we actually doing when we discriminate between people? How are we being influenced by society?

5. What is forgotten by those who give special treatment to the rich (verse 5)? What is true wealth?

6. What is done to the poor (verse 6)? What are the rich doing to the Christians? In both cases, what is the result (verse 7)?

♦ **7.** In verse 8, what quotation summarizes *the royal law?*

Why is applying this law important in our relationships to each other?

8. What happens if we show favoritism, and why (verses 9-10)?

9. What is the consequence of breaking even one point of the law? How is this illustrated (verses 10-11)?

♦ **10.** What lies ahead for every believer (verse 12)? Give specific examples of how this truth can motivate changes in our conversation and behavior.

11. How can we show mercy (instead of judgment) to members of our society and to fellow believers?

FAITH-FULL DEEDS

James 2:14-26

Living true to what we profess is not easy. It can be risky and inconvenient, but God promises his own Holy Spirit to help us. Desperate human needs surround us. What a magnificent framework of opportunity for Christians to demonstrate their faith. James urges us to spiritual maturity through a faith lived out in good works.

1. Relate an instance when someone's active help ministered more to you than words.

Read James 2:14-26.

    2. Who is James addressing in verse 14? What does he imply by his questions?

    3. Describe the kind of faith James is challenging. What example does he give to illustrate his point (verses 15-16)?

    4. What principle about faith does he give in verse 17? What motivates the believer to action?

    5. What objection might someone raise? How does James refute the attempt to separate faith and works (verse 18)?

◆ **6.** In verse 19, what point is James making?

◆ **7.** What illustration is given as evidence for James's assertions (verses 20-24)?

8. According to verses 21 and 23, on what basis was Abraham declared righteous before God? (See Genesis 22:1-12.)

9. What did Rahab's faith lead her to do? (For her story, read Joshua 2:1-24.)

10. According to verse 26, how do we know a body is alive? How can we tell the difference between genuine faith in Jesus Christ and a mere profession of orthodoxy?

11. What influence can an active faith have on people who don't know Jesus Christ?

12. Think of a specific way you can act out your faith to someone in need this week.

WATCHING OUR WORDS

James 3:1-12

"Think before you speak." How many times have we wished we could live by that simple maxim? It has become important in our culture to express feelings, and in the name of "honesty" we often blurt out hateful, hurting words. There is a time for loving honesty, but there is never a time to lash out and sin with our tongues. James takes a serious look at the trouble with our tongues and cautions us to watch our words.

1. Think of a time when you regretted something you said. How did you resolve it?

Read James 3:1-12.

♦ **2.** What warning does James give to aspiring teachers?

What might be some reasons for stricter judgment of teachers in the church?

3. Review what James has already said about speech in 1:19, 26. What is one characteristic of a spiritually mature person (verse 2)?

4. In verses 3-5 how does James illustrate the power of small things? How is a tongue like a bit and a rudder?

5. What common "speech problem" is referred to in verse 5? How can this cause great damage?

6. What metaphors about the tongue are listed in verse 6? How can a tongue not controlled by God "corrupt" the whole person?

7. From what source does the tongue's tremendous power for evil come? Whose power does this represent?

♦ **8.** Why can we not tame the tongue (verses 7-8)?

9. In verses 9-10, what good is the tongue capable of? What evil?

Who do we ultimately address in both blessing and cursing?

10. What is the main point of the illustrations in verses 11-12? Describe how our words can reveal what is in our soul.

11. Why do you think James gives so much attention to this problem?

12. What do you struggle with the most in controlling what you say? Pray specifically for each other in these areas.

HEAVENLY WISDOM

James 3:13-18

The *American Heritage Dictionary* defines wisdom as "an understanding of what is true, right or lasting." This is a worthy goal, but a biblical understanding of wisdom goes a bit further. James tells us that our knowledge of what is right must influence our behavior. Wisdom is more than having a profound insight or a correct response. It must also show itself in right living, leading to peaceful, loving relationships.

1. Think of a person you know who has real wisdom. How is that wisdom evident in his or her life?

Read James 3:13-18.

2. What is linked with wisdom in verse 13? What should be done with this knowledge?

3. What does James mean by living a "good life"?

◆ 4. Define *humility*. Why is "true wisdom" humble?

5. What underlying motives does counterfeit wisdom produce? With what results (verses 14, 16)?

6. How might envy or selfish ambition be exhibited in relationships or in the church?

7. In verse 15, what terms are used to describe counterfeit wisdom? Restate these terms in your own words.

8. What is the source of true wisdom (verse 17)?

9. What is the first and essential quality of godly wisdom? How does this quality relate to the ones that follow?

10. What attitudes toward others spring from holiness of character? In what situations can these attitudes be expressed?

11. What is the end result of true wisdom (verse 18)? Contrast this with the results of spurious wisdom in verse 16.

12. Do you recognize attitudes of jealousy and self-centeredness in yourself? How can you find true wisdom?

HUMBLE SUBMISSION

James 4:1-10

James has challenged us to persevere in difficult times and to exhibit our faith by living wisely. Now he shows us the key to sustaining this active, trusting faith. By humbling ourselves, recognizing our sin, and staying near to our loving God, we will see his grace working powerfully in us.

1. When you don't get something you want, how do you usually respond?

Read James 4:1-10.

2. Contrast the atmosphere of verse 1 with that of James 3:18. Who is fighting whom?

3. How can one believer "kill" another believer? What kinds of things do you covet?

4. What does James identify as the root cause within us for this hostility toward one another (verses 1-2)?

5. What kind of prayer does God "resist" (verse 3)? What is a *right* motive in prayer?

♦ **6.** What two friendships cannot coexist (verses 4-5)?

7. When we cherish a close relationship with those who exclude God and his will from their lives, what can happen to *our* relationship with God?

♦ **8.** How can the Christian live wholly for God in a corrupt world (verse 6)?

9. List the action verbs in verses 7-10. Why do you think submission is named first?

10. How may we actively cultivate fellowship with God (verses 7-8)?

11. What is involved in humbling ourselves before God (verses 8-10)?

12. What keeps you from submitting wholeheartedly to God? Pray that God would help you learn how to walk humbly with him.

KEEPING PERSPECTIVE

James 4:11–5:6

Blaise Pascal once noted that humanity lives in a state of "inconstancy, boredom, and anxiety." These feelings can result in a desperate attempt to pamper and control our own lives. In this passage James shows us how futile this effort is, and how much we need God's corrective grace in our lives to live in dependence on him and retain a true perspective of who we are and how we live.

1. What do you plan to be doing in the next five years?

Read James 4:11–5:6.

2. Compare 4:11 with James 1:26 and 3:9. What are some ways we speak against others?

◆ 3. When we criticize someone else, how does it follow that we are also judging the law?

4. Who is the law giver, and what power does he have (4:12)?

5. How does my right and authority to judge someone else compare with God's?

6. What does the person in 4:13 presume about his or her life?

7. Are making plans, buying, and selling legitimate pursuits in life? When do they become wrong?

8. How can we express our confidence that God is in control in our daily lives (4:15)? How should this affect our plans and actions?

9. Why is boasting, in this context, evil (4:16)?

10. What is the sin of 4:17? How can this knowledge relate to our planning?

11. What does James say is ahead for the rich (5:1-3)? How can wealth destroy people?

◆ **12.** Of what does James accuse the rich people (5:3-6)?

13. What truth in this study has the most relevance for your life now? Pray together for renewed dependence on God.

PATIENCE AND PRAYER

James 5:7-20

Realistic to the end, James brings his practical letter to a close. With the reality of Christ's return before us, he urges us to press on in our faith walk with patience and persistent prayer, knowing that our God is full of mercy and compassion.

1. What do you find yourself praying about the most?

Read James 5:7-20.

2. All through his letter James has talked about trials, pressures, problems, and injustices. In the light of these realities, what attitude should the Christian maintain (verses 7-8)? For how long?

3. Why would James inject the warning of verse 9?

4. How is Job an example for us of patience in suffering (verses 10-11)?

In all of life's experiences what does God want us to learn about himself?

5. What more do we learn about controlling the tongue from verse 12? (See Matthew 5:34-37.)

What does swearing accomplish?

6. In what areas of life are we to involve God (verses 13-14)? What are we acknowledging about God when we pray and praise?

7. Besides private prayer, what other resources do we have as believers (verses 14-16)?

◆ **8.** What can we ask of our spiritual leaders when we are in need?

◆ **9.** When we have sinned and need to be healed spiritually as well as physically, what can we do (verse 16)? Under what conditions can believers be open with one another?

10. What can prayer do (verses 16-17)? What happened when Elijah prayed?

11. If a Christian begins to turn from the truth, who is responsible to bring that person back? Why is this a privilege as well as a responsibility?

12. What in James's letter has been the greatest encouragement to you? What is the greatest personal challenge?

LEADER'S NOTES

Study 1/Joyful Perseverance

Question 3. *Christ* is Greek for the "anointed one" or Messiah. This showed that James believed Jesus to be the Messiah. *Lord* implies the sovereignty of God.

Question 4. This letter was written first to Jewish Christians who had been scattered beyond the borders of Palestine because of persecution. But in a broader sense it is sent to all true Christian believers who are "the Israel of God" (Galatians 6:16) by faith. Therefore this book is not a guide on how to become a Christian, but on how to achieve the goals of the Christian life under the stresses of present-day life.

Study 2/Steady Under Stress

Question 4. It is important to note that "[d]oubt is not the opposite of faith, nor is it the same as unbelief. Doubt is a state of mind in suspension *between* faith and unbelief so that it is neither of them wholly and it is each only partly" (Os Guinness, *In Two Minds,* p. 27. Downers Grove, Ill.: InterVarsity Press, 1976). And as such it can be a significant means of growth in our faith.

Question 9. "What is the crown? It is the *crown of life . . . the crown which consists of life;* the crown is life itself. The crown . . . [and] possession of the Christian is a new kind of life which is life indeed" (William Barclay, *The Letters of James and Peter,* p. 58. Edinburgh: Saint Andrew Press, 1958).

Question 13. *First fruits* is a term borrowed from the harvest, and implies that it is the first and finest of the gathered crop, and often the part that was offered as a sacrifice to God. Christians then can be examples of new birth and new life, with more of the spiritual harvest to follow.

Study 3/Listening and Doing

Question 6. James uses the phrase "the perfect law that gives freedom" to describe a particular function of the message Jesus had spoken to his disciples. Jesus said, "If you hold to my teaching, you are really my disciples. Then you will know the truth, and the truth will set you free" (John 8:31-32). When a person trusts in Christ, Christ's words become to that person not only a source of life, but a source of power. We are told not only what to do but we are given power by the Holy Spirit to do it.

James, knowing what Jesus said, informs us that we were born of the word of truth (James 1:18), we should accept the word planted in our hearts (verse 21), and we should listen to the word (verse 22), realizing that whoever obeys it will be blessed by God. When we think of law we think of restriction, but James sees the "law that gives freedom" as a guideline that the Christian is now able to follow by the power of Christ.

Question 10. The "world" refers to the "whole human scheme of things . . . without reference to God, his laws, his values or his ultimate judgment" (Alec Motyer, *The Message of James,* p. 77. Downers Grove, Ill.: InterVarsity Press, 1985). See James 4:4.

■ Study 4/Loving without Judging

Question 7. The "royal law" James describes here refers to the pattern of behavior expected of those who have become subjects in God's kingdom. See Matthew 22:36-40.

Question 10. It is clear in Scripture that believers, though assured of salvation, will be judged for their actions. See Romans 2:16; 14:10-13; 2 Corinthians 5:10; Revelation 20:11ff.

■ Study 5/Faith-Full Deeds

Question 6. "Every morning and evening the pious Jew recited the Shema, the opening words of which are 'Hear, O Israel, Jehovah our God, Jehovah is one.' This monotheism was a fundamental article of the creed. But merely giving assent to this without any resultant deeds lifts a man no higher than the level of 'devils' (demons) who believe the same. Their belief is clearly worthless and they 'tremble' (shudder) as they contemplate meeting the one God in judgment. Such faith, which might be described as mere intellectual belief, is not the faith that saves" (*The New Bible Commentary,* p. 1122).

Question 7. Some suppose Paul and James took opposite points of view regarding faith and works. When Paul says that the works of the law do not gain merit before God he places the emphasis on faith alone. James certainly believes in faith for salvation but adds that the proof of true faith will be practical good works. Both

Paul and James are emphasizing a transformed inner life. Paul says that the entrance into the transformed life is faith, not works. James says that the evidence of the transformed life is not intellectual faith alone, but is seen in active, loving, helpful deeds and attitudes.

■ Study 6/Watching Our Words

Question 2. "Teaching was a highly valued and respected profession in Jewish culture, and many Jews who embraced Christianity wanted to become teachers. James warned that although it is good to aspire to teach, the teachers' responsibility is great because their words and example affect others' spiritual lives" *(Life Application Bible, New International Version,* p. 2249. Wheaton, Ill.: Tyndale House Publishers, 1991).

Question 8. "If no human being can control the tongue, why bother trying? Even if we may not achieve perfect control of our tongues, we can still learn enough control to reduce the damage our words can do. It is better to fight a fire than to go around setting new ones! Remember that we are not fighting the tongue's fire in our own strength. The Holy Spirit will give us increasing power to monitor and control what we say, so that when we are offended, the Spirit will remind us of God's love, and we won't react in a hateful manner. When we are criticized, the Spirit will heal the hurt, and we won't lash out" *(Life Application Bible,* p. 2249).

■ Study 7/Heavenly Wisdom

Question 4. Jesus spoke of himself as "gentle and humble" (Matthew 11:29). Humility is not weakness but a willing acceptance of the control of God without self-assertion. For the Christian it means always being teachable, having the attitude, "I have more to learn," in contrast to arrogance and self-importance.

▪ Study 8/Humble Submission

Question 6. James 4:5 is a difficult verse to decipher, and many commentators differ in their conclusions. James is not quoting a specific passage, and it is unclear if "the spirit he caused to live in us" refers to our spirit, the breath of life as such, that envies wrongly, or to the Holy Spirit in us who is yearning jealously. J.B. Phillips states verse 5 thus: "Or do you think what the scriptures have to say about this is a mere formality? Do you imagine that this spirit of passionate jealousy is the Spirit he has caused to live in us? Yet he gives us grace which is stronger" (J. B. Phillips, *The New Testament in Modern English, Revised.* New York: MacMillan Publishing Co., 1972).

Question 8. God's grace is the undeserved power of God given to effectively strengthen the Christian.

▪ Study 9/Keeping Perspective

Question 3. When we slander or defame another, we are actually defaming and judging the law. "The speaker implies superior knowledge and an independent position, as if he himself were not under the law. When he ought to be a doer of the law by obeying it, he is putting himself above it as well as above his brother. He has made himself a *judge* . . . [and] a *lawgiver.* He has really set up another law by which he judges his brother . . . . [and] arrogantly usurps [God's] position" (*New Bible Commentary, Revised,* p. 1233).

Question 12. The "day of slaughter" here may refer to the judgment of the Lord. See Jeremiah 12:3; 25:34.

■ Study 10/Patience and Prayer

Question 8. In Bible times oil was used for medicinal purposes (see Isaiah 1:6 and Luke 10:34). It is also used in praying for healing as a symbol of the Holy Spirit's power.

Question 9. James is not encouraging indiscriminate confession. It is a serious thing to confide honestly a deep need or sin to someone else. It is also a serious thing to receive such a confidence and pray about it together. There must be trust and love.

WHAT SHOULD WE STUDY NEXT?

To help your group answer that question, we've listed the Fisherman Guides by category so you can choose your next study.

TOPICAL STUDIES

Becoming Women of Purpose, Barton

Building Your House on the Lord, Brestin

Discipleship, Reapsome

Doing Justice, Showing Mercy, Wright

Encouraging Others, Johnson

Examining the Claims of Jesus, Brestin

Friendship, Brestin

The Fruit of the Spirit, Briscoe

Great Doctrines of the Bible, Board

Great Passages of the Bible, Plueddemann

Great People of the Bible, Plueddemann

Great Prayers of the Bible, Plueddemann

Growing Through Life's Challenges, Reapsome

Guidance & God's Will, Stark

Higher Ground, Brestin

How Should a Christian Live? (1,2, & 3 John), Brestin

Marriage, Stevens

Moneywise, Larsen

One Body, One Spirit, Larsen

The Parables of Jesus, Hunt

Prayer, Jones

The Prophets, Wright

Proverbs & Parables, Brestin

Relationships, Hunt

Satisfying Work, Stevens & Schoberg

Senior Saints, Reapsome

Sermon on the Mount, Hunt

The Ten Commandments, Briscoe

When Servants Suffer, Rhodes

Who Is Jesus? Van Reken

Worship, Sibley

BIBLE BOOK STUDIES

Genesis, Fromer & Keyes

Job, Klug

Psalms, Klug

Proverbs: Wisdom That Works, Wright

Ecclesiastes, Brestin

Jonah, Habakkuk, & Malachi, Fromer & Keyes

Matthew, Sibley

Mark, Christensen

Luke, Keyes

John: Living Word, Kuniholm

Acts 1-12, Christensen

Paul (Acts 13-28), Christensen

Romans: The Christian Story, Reapsome

1 Corinthians, Hummel

Strengthened to Serve (2 Corinthians), Plueddemann

Galatians, Titus & Philemon, Kuniholm

Ephesians, Baylis

Philippians, Klug

Colossians, Shaw

Letters to the Thessalonians, Fromer & Keyes

Letters to Timothy, Fromer & Keyes

Hebrews, Hunt

James, Christensen

1 & 2 Peter, Jude, Brestin

How Should a Christian Live? (1, 2 & 3 John), Brestin

Revelation, Hunt

BIBLE CHARACTER STUDIES

Ruth & Daniel, Stokes

David: Man after God's Own Heart, Castleman

Job, Klug

King David: Trusting God for a Lifetime, Castleman

Elijah, Castleman

Men Like Us, Heidebrecht & Scheuermann

Peter, Castleman

Paul (Acts 13-28), Christensen

Great People of the Bible, Plueddemann

Women Like Us, Barton

Women Who Achieved for God, Christensen

Women Who Believed God, Christensen